this blessed land

by Gene Dekovic

Illuminations Press — St. Helena, California

The Robert Mondavi Winery
— *interacting with nature to nurture wines to greatness*

Books by Gene Dekovic

Self Reliance
Vita Italiana
Love One Another
This Blessed Land

Library of Congress Catalog Number: 80-84495
ISBN 0-937088-00-5 (hardbound)
ISBN 0-937088-01-3 (softbound)

Manufactured in the United States of America

1 2 3 4 5 6 7 8 9 10

contents

INTRODUCTION

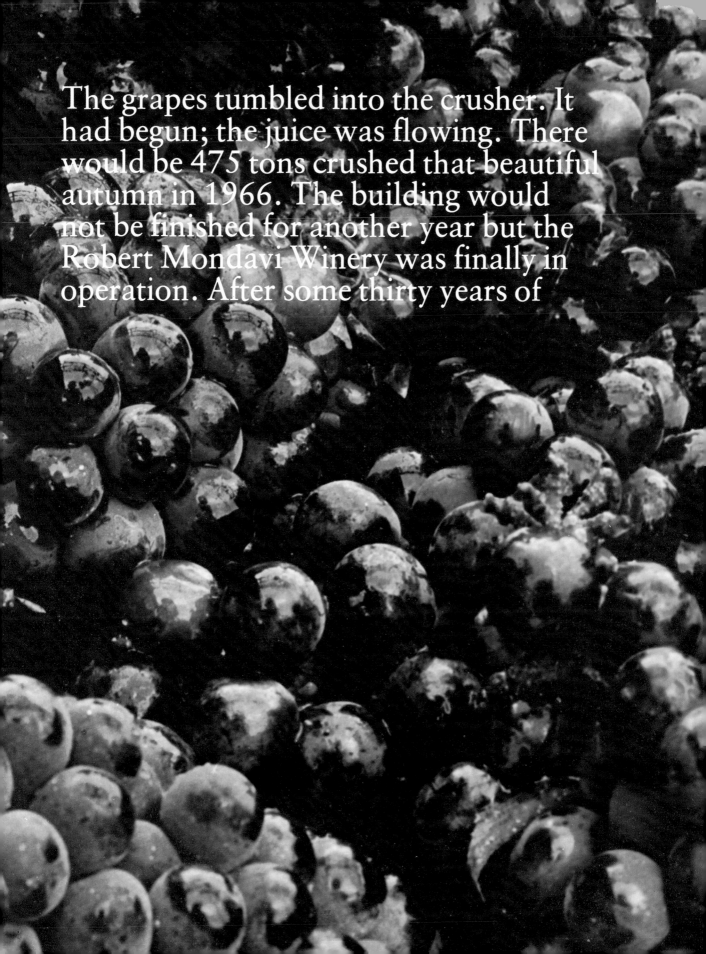

The grapes tumbled into the crusher. It had begun; the juice was flowing. There would be 475 tons crushed that beautiful autumn in 1966. The building would not be finished for another year but the Robert Mondavi Winery was finally in operation. After some thirty years of developing quality wines in the family business, the Charles Krug Winery, Robert Mondavi was on the way toward his goal — to make great wines, classic wines, wines that would compete favorably with the best the world could produce.

To make the best wines in the world would take time, a lot of time. The proper style would have to be developed. Many techniques would need to be tested. The wines would need to age — in the barrel and then in the bottle. To help Robert with this work and to carry on his program was his older son, Michael. Later, his younger son, Tim, and daughter, Marcia, would decide that they too shared their father's goal.

Since then, all of the younger Mondavis have worked in every phase of the winemaking process, from washing tanks and barrels and shoveling pomace to doing the laboratory work and the tasting required to decide what needs to be done to a wine for it to achieve its potential. Their experience qualified them to take on larger responsibilities as the winery has grown.

Now, after fourteen years in production and marketing, Michael is President of the winery and responsible for all operations. Marcia is Vice President of Eastern Operations, representing the winery to the important markets in the east, and Tim is Vice President of Production, responsible for everything involved in the making of the wines. Tim is the "winemaker", which is the key responsibility in a winery. Wineries live and die by the results of their winemakers' decisions. Tim Mondavi is carrying on the traditions established by his father and his brother during their years as winemakers.

Robert Mondavi is now Chairman. Freed of the responsibility for day to day operations, Robert is able to channel his energies into the long-range development of the winery and breaking new ground in developing classic wines.

Michael, Marcia, Robert and Tim Mondavi are shown at right attending the opening of an art exhibit in the winery's Vineyard Room. One of the most active places in the valley, the Vineyard Room hosts community meetings, civic events, and private gatherings. It is also a cultural focal point with musical and theatrical performances and exhibits of the work of outstanding artists. Cooking seminars have been conducted there by great chefs of the world and during the summer the evening breezes carry the jazz strains of Ella Fitzgerald, Stan Getz, Joe Pass, Oscar Peterson, and other masters to sold out audiences. The concerts are benefits for local hospitals and the cost of admission is high, yet the mixture of the summer environment, picnicking on the lawn, winetasting, and superb music is irresistible. The audiences and the community find the winery to be a most sociable neighbor.

Wine is very complex. One of the most complex of all foods, it contains several hundred different compounds. And no two wines can be alike unless their complexity and character have been filtered out. It is not possible to make the same wine two years in a row. The same vines and the same procedures will produce a similar wine the second year. The wine will be similar in style, in body and in color, but it will not be the same wine. There will be a difference; a difference that will be detected by the palate.

These differences between wines from year to year are important to Robert

Mondavi. He does not blend them out, for they add to the wine drinker's pleasure. Each wine adds another experience to the memory. As the wine drinker's memory stores more and more different wine experiences, the palate becomes ever more sensitive and each new wine is experienced ever more fully.

All of the winemaking operations are guided by Robert Mondavi's basic belief that each varietal wine should have a distinctive style with maximum complexity and vintage distinction. The objective is to provide the wine drinker, beginner or widely experienced, with a maximum reward in color, aroma, bouquet and taste.

In these pages, you will be brought into the winemaking operations from dormant vines through bottle aging and on to the enjoyment of wine with food. There are no secret steps or formulae. Each wine is a product of the winemaker's judgments. Time and temperature are the winemaker's instruments. As the composer arranges musical notes and intervals to create melodies and rhythms, the winemaker orchestrates his work of art by controlling the temperature and time in every step of the way to wine: in fermentation, in skin contact, in aging vats, in oak cooperage, and in the bottle. Each step, each movement in the process is based upon the winemaker's judgment of the wine.

The winemaker's judgment is the crucial dimension. Nothing can replace it. The fully equipped laboratory makes daily tests. Sophisticated equipment and techniques measure quantities of particular elements. It is very exacting work and very important but no laboratory test can tell the winemaker that it is time to move the wine to the next stage. Only the palate can provide the information necessary for that decision.

Every wine is tasted many times. Samples are tasted daily during fermentation and then less frequently as the wine moves into the lengthy aging period. In making the critical decisions, the winemaker uses the same tools that the wine drinkers use in enjoying wine — the eyes, the nose, and the palate. The tools that have been used since wine was discovered eons ago are still the only measure of wine.

A modern winery is filled with highly efficient machines for crushing grapes, for pressing the juice from the skins, and for moving wine quickly and cleanly when it needs to be moved. The wines of today are much improved because of the machines that are available. Oxidation has been prevented or minimized at every step; the wines are fresher and better tasting. But these are mechanical procedures; the machines do what has been done for centuries, they just do it faster. The machines cannot make great wine. Great wines come from a human process; individuals using their sensory equipment to make fine discriminations. Great wines come from people appraising the colors, the aromas, the bouquets, the tastes.

This book could not portray the essence of the winemaking process. What happens day by day and month after month in the fermentation tanks, in the oak casks and barrels, and in the bottles is beyond the camera lens and beyond the language of the lay writer. Even the chemist cannot detail some of the events occurring in the wine. But this book can and does portray people at work, people doing the things that make it possible for the unseen events to take place.

The people working in the winery are not just earning their living, they are very involved in what they are doing. Their involvement in making wine is very visible. Wine is very special to them; they will talk about it for hours, collect it, drink it. They are aware that the difference between a fine quality wine and a mediocre wine can often lie in what they do — in how the wine is moved from one container to another, in the care taken in making readings, in cleaning the equipment, in all of the operations. The work atmosphere is quite different from the worker detachment found in some other industries.

The involvement with wine and winemaking is contagious. Sons and daughters follow fathers and mothers, brothers and sisters follow one another into university programs and then into wineries. Wine people marry and make wine at home. The wine country is filled with wine families.

One of the families of wine workers involved in and dedicated to making great wine is the Robert Mondavi family. Michael, Tim, and Marcia have acquired Robert's determination to make great wines. As everyone else in the winery, they are imbued with Robert's determination, which he expressed quite succinctly, "We have been developing our character and it's not easy. It takes total involvement; total dedication."

Robert's total involvement comes from his conviction that he is making wine in the best location in the world. Here are the right soils for the great grapes and here is the almost ideal climate, the single most important element in making great wine. All climates take unpredictable turns; extreme winds, rain, or cold at critical times exact a terrible toll on agricultural crops. The Napa Valley has had such times and the damage has been extensive but, of all of the prime grape growing regions in the world, the Napa Valley has the most consistent climatic conditions for producing mature grapes year after year. Differences occur from year to year but practically every year is a vintage year in that the winemakers have mature grapes to crush. Mature grapes — with high sugar and high acid — are essential if one is to make great wine. To have them year after year makes the Napa Valley "this blessed land."

ONE | THE VINE IS THE BEGINNING

Great wine can be made anywhere —
given great grapes. Great grapes, however, can be found in only a few places
in the world. They are very demanding.
They require proper soil, suitable terrain,
and adequate moisture at certain times but,
most of all, they need a special climate.

the warming sun disturbs winter's sleep; buds
expand and burst outward in a frenzy of energy

It is the beginning of May and the vines continue their rapid growth. The flower buds are forming and the shoots expand in all directions; as the afternoon sun increases its warmth the shoots will grow an inch a day. It is an amazing process. The vineyard literally gets greener by the hour.

Twenty-six inches of rain had fallen during the dormant period. Another two inches have fallen since the bud break in April and by the middle of May the rain will end, a total of thirty inches for the season, just three inches shy of the average rainfall. The ground has its moisture and now the clouds will leave and the sun will do its work.

Three and a half months of clear, sunny days with the highs averaging eighty-five degrees and cool nights down in the fifties; these are the ideal conditions for raising great grapes. And there are enough variations from these averages throughout the Napa Valley to accommodate the varying needs of different grape varieties.

Based on the heat-summation system developed by the Enology Department of the University of California at Davis, the Napa Valley has three climatic regions. The southern part of the valley is cooled by the breezes of San Francisco Bay and its summer climate is very similar to the climate of northern Europe. This area is ideal for the early ripening Pinot Noir, Chardonnay and Johannisberg Riesling.

Further inland the temperature warms. From Oakville to just north of St. Helena, the average daily temperature is about five degrees warmer during the growing period. This region is better suited to Cabernet Sauvignon, Sauvignon Blanc, and Zinfandel. The northern part of the valley is the warmest. This is classified as a zone three. It averages the additional five degrees per day that Gamay and Petite Sirah need to achieve full maturity.

Of course, there are more than just the temperatures at play. The variations in terrain which affect drainage, the varying exposure of the vines to the sun, and the differences in soils are all factors in determining which vine will do best in any given location. The interactions between terrain and all of the weather variables are responsible for distinctive climatic changes within very small areas. These micro-climates produce differences within the grapes. In some cases, vines growing within fifty yards of each other will bear grapes with quite different characteristics — sugar, acids, flavors, intensity of flavors and maturity dates will vary considerably.

It is clear that every change in water, in temperature, in sunshine, and in soil has some effect on the quality of the crop. There is also a difference in the character of the crop. Since no two growing seasons can ever have the same pattern of rain, sunshine, winds, and temperatures, no two crops can ever be the same. Every year the wine will possess some distinction as a result of the season's particular weather pattern. These distinctions in the wines can be removed by blending or they can be retained and fully developed in the wine-making process. Robert Mondavi believes that these vintage distinctions should be fully developed to provide maximum pleasure to the wine drinker. Each year's wine has its own distinctions in addition to its basic Robert Mondavi character.

Color in the Vineyard

The vineyards portray a varied and changing spectrum
from winter's yellow waves of wild mustard to the vibrant
colors of spring growth and the greenery of summer leaves
to the lush golds and intense blues of Chardonnay and
Cabernet Sauvignon at season's end.

About eight weeks after the buds break open, the vines will flower for a week or two and then the grape clusters begin to form. By the third week of June, the grapes are well formed. The grapes will continue to grow for the next two months and then will begin to change color in August. The bright greens will change to reddish blue or yellow. During the growing period, the amount of sugar in the grape is very low and the acidity is high. The changing of the color indicates the end of the growing and the beginning of the ripening. From then on, the amount of sugar will increase and the acidity decrease until the point when the winemaker decides the grapes are to be harvested and crushed.

Great wine grapes are small and intense in flavor. The intensity is achieved by limiting the number of vines per acre and by extensive pruning of each vine during the dormant period. The vines are spaced six to eight feet apart in rows twelve feet apart. Planted closer together with more vines per acre, the intensity would be reduced. Without pruning, the crop would increase but maturity would be delayed and the sugars and acids would be reduced. Larger grapes could be produced by watering the vines during the growing season but the larger grapes will produce a watery wine, weak in flavor. As a consequence, the yield per acre of great wine grapes is much, much less than the bulk wine grapes or table grapes. Cabernet Sauvignon yields four to six tons of grapes per acre while Carignane, Grenache, and French Colombard will yield nine to fourteen tons.

Seven years are required to achieve a fully producing vineyard. The first year is occupied with preparing the land. The rootstock is planted the second year. Because grapevines are vulnerable to a large number of diseases, the grower usually plants cuttings certified to be free of known virus diseases by the California Department of Agriculture. When the rootstock has been in the ground a season, the variety can be grafted to it. Rootstock is used because it is less susceptible to injury by root parasites than are the roots of the varietal grapes.

Two years after the grafting, the vines will bear a small crop — a fifth to a third of the ultimate normal crop. Another year and the crop will increase to somewhat over a half and the following year almost a full crop can be expected. The eighth year brings the full crop. Meanwhile the grower has been cultivating, irrigating, and training the vines every year. A vineyard represents a significant investment in labor and materials and a considerable faith in the ability to predict that there will be a market for the particular varietal wine almost a decade into the future.

Almost half of the grapes the winery crushes in making its varietal wines are grown in the Robert Mondavi Vineyards. There are two, with a total of 1100 acres of premium varietal grapes. The To-Kalon Vineyard surrounds the winery and extends southward over 600 acres along the base of the Mayacamas Mountains on the west side of the Napa Valley. Because of the mountains, winds, temperatures, and rainfall vary throughout the vineyard. The changes in terrains and soils create additional differences. Instead of a single climate best suited to a single grape variety, there are several climates. The conditions are better suited to several varieties. Much experimentation has resulted in highly productive plantings of the great grapes — Cabernet Sauvignon, Sauvignon Blanc, Johannisberg Riesling and Chenin Blanc.

green leaves and the summer sun;
photosynthesis at work —
converting carbon dioxide and water
into energy-rich compounds

Virus? Fungus? Bacteria? Healthy? The microbiologist cuts and probes and observes.

The Oak Knoll Vineyard, some eight miles to the southeast, is on the other side of the valley and in a cooler climate region. This vineyard also contains a range of conditions in terrains and soils and weather, making some sections better suited to one grape variety than another. Here in areas providing what each needs are also the great grapes — Chardonnay, Pinot Noir, Sauvignon Blanc, Cabernet Sauvignon, Merlot and Johannisberg Riesling.

The vineyards are tended by people of two cultures. The microbiologists and viticulture majors with advanced degrees from the universities approach the vines from a scientific perspective. Their language is heavy with the terms of biology and chemistry. They are concerned with cloning and the culture of the grapes, the prevention and curing of diseases, and all other matters affecting the productivity and quality of the vine's output.

The other culture is concerned with the vine and its output also but the approach is intuitive and the vocabulary is less technical. These are the vineyard workers. Mostly men of Mexican descent, many have spent all of their adult lives working in the vineyards and acquiring knowledge and skills. Along with their expertise, they developed a love of the land and the grape. They are in their element out in the vineyards.

The winged, double cluster of Chardonnay grapes shown at left is almost ready for harvesting. Chardonnay and Pinot Noir are early ripening grapes and are usually the first to be harvested in the Napa Valley. These are the two great grapes of the French provinces of Burgundy and Champagne. Pinot Noir is the grape of the great red Burgundy wines and Chardonnay is the grape of the famous white Burgundy wines — Chablis, Montrachet, Meursault, Pouilly-Fuissé, and others. And both grapes are responsible for the world renowned sparkling wines of Champagne.

Chardonnay and Pinot Noir are also great grapes in the Napa Valley. They have retained their distinguishing characteristics in their new home and, when handled properly, they yield wines of comparable quality. As with all fine varietal wines in California, the name of the grape is also the name of the wine. This differs from the French and others whose wines were long ago identified by their place of origin. The name of the grape is not used. Most people in France who drink Chablis are not familiar with the name of the grape that made the wine. This system of place naming would not work in California since almost all of the quality wineries produce more than one variety of wine. The pattern of grape growing varies with the climate and soil conditions and every grape growing area raises two or more varieties.

Thus, in California, a fine wine is identified by the variety of grape, the area or region of the vineyard, and the producer of the wine. All three are relevant to the selection of a wine, for a variety of grapevine will not produce grapes and wine of constant quality or character in all locations and there are differences between wine-makers in their handling of the grape. There are Chardonnays of comparable quality and cost that differ widely in character. One is light and delicate and possesses great finesse and another is big and robust.

There are wines produced in California that carry the names of places in Europe such as Burgundy, Chablis, Sauternes, Rhine, etc. The overwhelming majority of California wines are in this group. These are the inexpensive wines made in the styles of their

the taste, the feel, the mature grape, the bunch; indications of the wine to come

the refractometer reads 22° sugar;
the time for picking approaches

namesakes. Known as generic wines, they are usually blends of many grapes, especially grapes which provide large yields but do not have distinctive flavors. Sold in large jugs as well as in bottles, these wines are comparable to the ordinary wines of Europe. But they are usually of much better quality than the typical "vin ordinaire" because they are made in large modern wineries under controlled conditions.

Cabernet Sauvignon and Sauvignon Blanc are two other great grapes that thrive in Napa Valley and produce great wines. Both of these grapes have lengthy and noble histories of producing great red and white wines of Bordeaux in France. In addition, Sauvignon Blanc is the grape of the fine white wines of Sancerre and Pouilly in the Loire Valley of France.

In the Napa Valley, Cabernet Sauvignon finds ideal climate and soil conditions. A late ripening grape, it is picked between the middle of October and early November. The small, very seedy berries in small clusters are intense with flavor, producing a wine long considered the king of red wines when allowed to age fully. A distant cousin, the white Sauvignon Blanc also finds its home in the clay soils and warm climate. For many years in California this grape was used solely to make sweet dessert wines, similar to the French Sauternes. Robert Mondavi believed the Sauvignon Blanc grape had other talents and proved it by developing a dry wine of great character. Full-bodied with a distinctive varietal aroma and golden color, the wine reflects a happy marriage of fruit and oak. To differentiate this dry wine from the sweet Sauvignon Blanc wines, Robert Mondavi originated the name Fumé Blanc, which indicated a relationship to the dry Pouilly Fumé and Sancerre wines of the Loire Valley.

The great Riesling grape of Alsace and the Rhine and Mosel in Germany has also found a nourishing home in the Napa Valley. This vigorous vine is not prolific; its small clusters of juicy and aromatic berries yield only four to six tons per acre but produce a wine of distinction with a light, fragrant softness and a fine flowery bouquet.

Chenin Blanc and Petite Sirah have come into prominence in recent years as vintners began using them as varietal grapes instead of as blending grapes. Robert Mondavi was the first to produce a Chenin Blanc wine. Since then, Chenin Blanc has become one of the most widely planted white varietal grapes in California. The Robert Mondavi Chenin Blanc is a mellow wine, moderately sweet with a delightful bouquet. Petite Sirah, like its counterparts in France's Rhone Valley, produces a big, inky purple, robust wine. The grape is very high in tannin, giving the wine a long life.

Just the opposite takes place with the Gamay grape. Its best wines are enjoyed young and fresh. The grape has a long history. Brought to France by the Romans, it has traveled to the Napa Valley without any loss in quality. A late maturing grape, the Gamay is generally harvested at the end of October. A short fermentation and then the wine is separated from the skins and seeds. There is color and good fruit flavor but little tannin; after six to eight months aging in oak and then bottled, the wine will soon be ready for full enjoyment.

The Zinfandel grape has a different story. Its past is shrouded in mystery. Long considered to be California's own grape, it is now believed to come from a clone of the Italian Primitivo grape. A versatile grape, Zinfandel can make wines light in color and body,

which should be drunk young, like the Gamay, or big wines, heavy with tannin which will be velvety and rich with complexity after several decades of aging. Robert Mondavi makes Zinfandel in the style of a Cabernet Sauvignon. With a year and a half or more of barrel aging, the wine has a dark ruby color, good body and a complex nose. It continues to improve with bottle age.

Now it is September. The Chardonnay, Pinot Noir, Sauvignon Blanc, Johannisberg Riesling, Cabernet Sauvignon and the other grapes have been tended all summer. The moisture has been controlled, the diseases have been combatted, the ground has been cultivated; now the grapes are approaching maturity and the vineyards have been busy with winemakers inspecting and tasting the grapes. Now the vineyards are filled with pickers.

The Chardonnay is ready; the sugar is up to 23 percent. The pickers arrive and begin their work now that the sun has evaporated the dew. The men work fast. The curved knife is sharp and there is a steady dropping of clusters as each man moves into the vine and buries his fast moving hands beneath the foliage, locating the clusters and cutting them loose.

When full, the lug box is hoisted and carried to the nearby gondola. Often, the lug box is transferred to the outstretched hands of a fellow worker in the next row who dumps its load into the gondola. There is a great amount of teamwork and camaraderie between the men. The continuous talk adds spice to the work. The men work in teams of 12 and they will fill a gondola with 4½ tons in less than 2 hours. The knives are sharpened frequently.

There are mechanical harvesters, large machines which straddle a row of vines and remove the grapes with banks of flexible rods which strike and shake the vines. The machines are able to pick a vineyard much faster than several crews of hand pickers and they are able to pick at night. But the vines must be trained through special pruning for several years before the machine can be used and even then there is a fair amount of damage to vines. Also, there are grape varieties which are difficult to harvest and must be picked by hand in order to collect all of the fruit. These limitations are quickly cancelled out, however, when weather conditions cause several varieties of grapes to ripen at the same time. Then the mechanical harvesters back up the picking crews and the grapes are picked while they are at their peak. The machines do the essential job but the great grapes and the great grapevines fare best in the hands of man.

Also, the vineyards need a rather large staff of workers the year round. The ground must be tilled, cover crops need to be turned over, weeds have to be cut, new plantings must be made and new vines need to be budded and trained. And, during the harvest season, crews of experienced workers are invaluable.

The time between picking and crushing is crucial. Once picked, great grapes do not remain great very long. That is why wineries are found out in the vineyards and not in urban locations. During the harvest season there is a steady stream of single gondolas pulled by pickup trucks or tractors coming into the winery yard. As soon as the gondola is loaded, it leaves for the winery. It would be more fuel efficient to wait until additional gondolas were full and pull several of them in one trip to the winery but the grapes would suffer and so would the wine.

The grapes move off to the winery. The pickers sharpen their knives as another tractor pulls the next gondola down the row to where the men are waiting.

38

The grapes are at the winery. Crush them now! This is the only imperative. After the grapes are crushed, the winemaker's choices are almost infinite. The art begins.

the giant screw moves the grapes into
the crusher-stemmer; a half-ton a minute

Flowing into a stainless steel fermentation tank, the surging mix of skins, seeds, pulp, and juice begins the rather simple process of changing from the juice of the grape into wine. The process is simple in that there are only eight to ten operations and most of them consist in moving the wine from one container to another. The process is not simple in how and when these operations are executed.

There are two procedures generally followed in making dry table wines, one for whites and another for reds. They both begin with the mixture of skins, seeds, pulp, and juice, called "must", that comes out of the crusher-stemmer. Now the first decision must be made; the amount of time the juice and the solids will remain together; will be "left on the skins" in the language of the winemaker.

The flavor of wine comes from the skins of the grapes. The color also comes from the skins. Tannin, the compound that preserves the wine and allows it to age with great benefit, comes from the seeds as well as the skins. The winemaker must decide for each batch of grapes how long the seeds and skins will remain with the juice. For white wines, it is usually a matter of hours. For red wines it is much longer, three to five days during fermentation and, for Cabernet Sauvignon, another ten to fifteen days after fermentation is completed.

The difference between a few or many hours for white wines depends upon the character of the grapes and the kind of wine to be made. Johannisberg Riesling and Chenin Blanc will remain on the skins for some three hours and Sauvignon Blanc and Chardonnay will remain in holding tanks with skins and seeds for six to eighteen hours. As with the red wines, the exact amount of time that the wine is left on the skins is a matter of the winemaker's judgment. He and his enologists are guided by what is required for the kind of wine to be made but they must also be open to the characteristics of the particular batch. They must be sensitive to the grape.

The "must" is separated in a wine press. The solids, called "pomace", are removed and returned to the vineyard to feed the soil. The pressing of the must is divided into several stages. The juice that flows as the skin of each grape is broken in the crusher-stemmer is called the "free run". The free run is the best of the juice and is usually kept apart for blending with the best juices from the pressing. The pressing involves a sequence of pressures applied to the must and as the pressure increases, the juice begins to contain seed tannins and other extractions which detract from the taste of the wine. These juices from the heavier pressings are not used for the varietal wines.

After pressing, the white wine juice is then cooled and circulated through the centrifuge which uses exaggerated gravity to remove any unwanted solids remaining in the juice. After this clarification, the juice is transferred to a fermenting tank and inoculated with a selected yeast culture.

Fermentation is the conversion of sugars to alcohols. It is the process that changes juice into wine. The selection of the particular strain of yeast to be used to ferment a batch of juice into wine is the second big decision the winemaker must make. It was Louis Pasteur who discovered that wine ferments because of wild yeasts which bloom on the skins of

carbon dioxide bubbles up, heat is generated;
actions and reactions in wine in fermentation

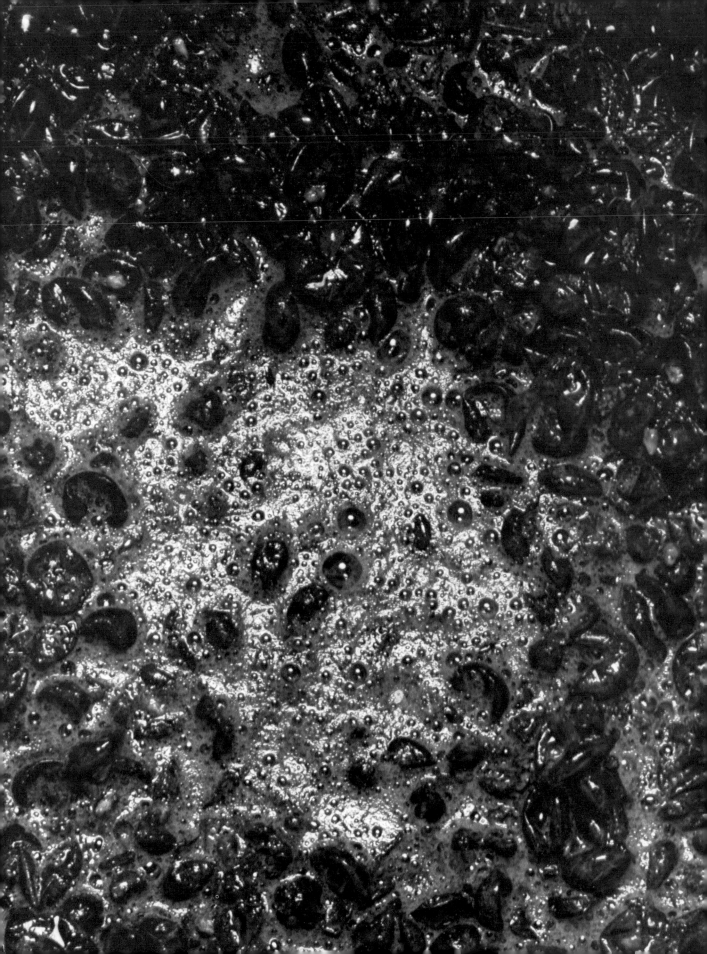

grapes. The yeasts feed on the sugar in the grape and create alcohol. Wild yeasts had been fermenting wine naturally for thousands of years — sometimes with very, very good results but also many times with results that were not pleasant. Many species of wild yeasts are killed off by a small amount of alcohol, stopping fermentation long before it is completed.

Since winemakers cannot rely on the wild yeasts, they replace them with pure cultures developed expressly for that purpose. Pasteur also discovered that yeasts could be isolated and would develop pure cultures; his contributions to winemaking in France and all of the world are inestimable. Today, winemakers have a great number of pure yeast cultures available to them. Each yeast is selected for its particular effect on a grape variety according to the winemaker's desired results. There is a great amount of experimentation being conducted today and there is much secrecy between many winemakers on what strains of yeasts are being used.

The next big decision the winemaker faces is the temperature of the fermentation. If allowed to continue unchecked, the heat will rise until the yeast can no longer function and the fermentation becomes "stuck". Winemakers traditionally controlled the temperature of the fermentation by natural means. Either the weather was cool or the fermentation vats were located in deep cellars or caves. White wines need to be fermented at much lower temperatures than red wines. Consequently, there were very few high quality white wines made in warm climates; all of the great white wines originated in the colder climates of Germany, France, and northern Italy.

Stainless steel tanks with cooling jackets now make it possible to maintain a close control of temperature during fermentation. The winemaker can select the exact temperature that will bring about the characteristics that are desired in the wine. The ideal in California for retaining the natural fruitiness and freshness in white wines is a three-to four-week fermentation at 50-55 degrees Fahrenheit. Robert Mondavi ferments Johannisberg Riesling at that temperature but his Chardonnay and Fumé Blanc are fermented at a higher temperature, 60-65 degrees, for two to three weeks. He believes the warmer fermentation retains the fine varietal characteristics while developing complexity in the aroma.

Another decision the winemaker faces is the type of container used for fermentation. Stainless steel is fine for light, fruity white wines, such as Johannisberg Riesling and Chenin Blanc but the complex, full-bodied whites, Fumé Blanc and Chardonnay, benefit greatly from part of the fermentation taking place in small oak barrels. Judgments must be made as to how much of each wine should ferment in oak and the amount of time each portion spends in stainless steel and in oak.

There are two basic differences in the red wine production procedures. First, the fermentation of red wines includes the skins and the seeds and these solids need to be distributed throughout the liquid to extract the required amount of flavor and color. The constantly rising carbon dioxide works against this distribution by carrying the solids up to the top of the tank where they pack tightly into a dense cap. This cap must be broken. This is done several times a day by an operation aptly called a "pumpover". The liquid juices are drawn off at the bottom of the tank and pumped over the top, sending the skins and seeds swirling throughout the fermenting wine.

Concentration. The silence is intense
with purpose. Color, aroma, taste—
the points for decision.

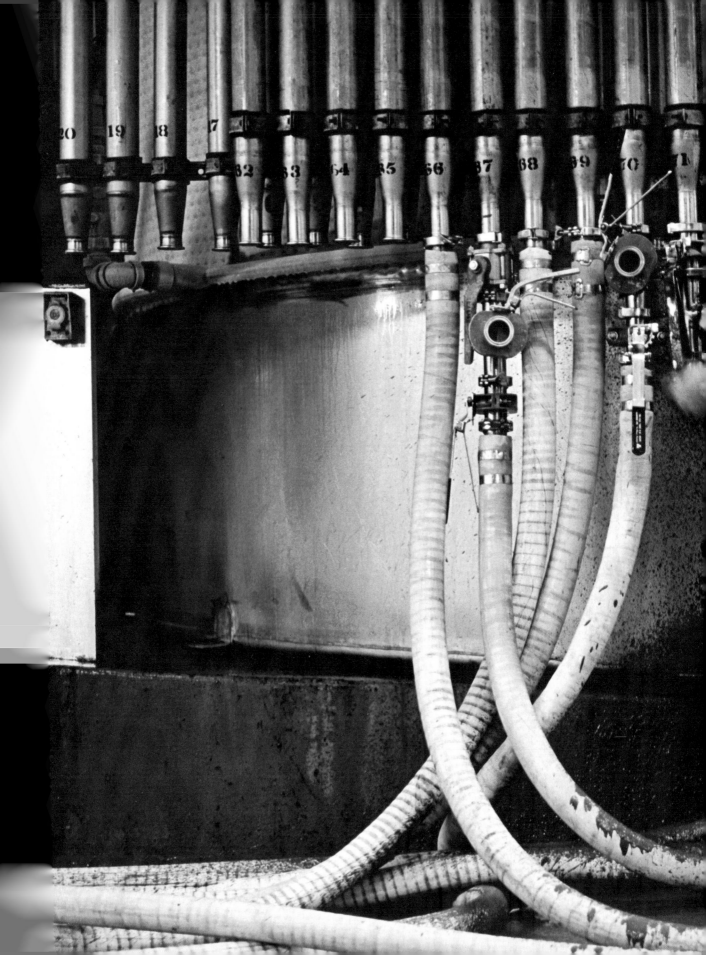

Another method for keeping the skins and seeds distributed throughout the liquid during red wine fermentation is the roto-tank. This is a 4,000 gallon horizontal tank which can be rotated a few revolutions per minute. This gentle movement continuously distributes the skins and solids throughout the fermenting juice and very delicately extracts flavor, color, and tannin from them.

The second difference in the production of red wine is the temperature of the fermentation. Red wines are fermented at much higher temperatures. Most California winemakers ferment their red wines at 70-75 degrees Fahrenheit but Robert Mondavi again prefers the results achieved from higher temperatures. He ferments the wines that should be aged — Cabernet Sauvignon, Pinot Noir, Petite Sirah and Zinfandel — at 80-88 degrees to achieve the fullness and complexity he wants in these wines. The light red wine, Napa Gamay, is the exception; it is partially fermented at 80 degrees and then separated from the skins to finish fermenting at a much cooler 65 degrees. This keeps the wine light and fresh, to be consumed while it is young. Fermented at the cooler temperature for a shorter period, the wine does not extract the compounds that require extended aging for maximum development. Napa Gamay is a simpler wine, providing a different experience.

In addition to fermenting the other red wines at higher temperatures, Robert Mondavi also keeps Cabernet Sauvignon in contact with the skins for another ten to fifteen days after the fermentation is completed. This extended skin contact develops additional body and varietal characteristics. The result is a fullness and a richness that could not be achieved by fermenting at the lower temperatures and reducing the time the wine is left on the skins.

At some point after the fermentation has begun, a secondary fermentation occurs in red wines. This is the malo-lactic fermentation. It is caused by lactic acid bacteria converting malic acid to lactic acid. In the process, carbon dioxide is given off. The effect of this fermentation is a softening and an increase of complexity of the wine because the acid content has been reduced by about half. It is important that the malo-lactic fermentation takes place sometime before bottling. If it takes place after bottling, the carbon dioxide that is generated in the process will make the wine gassy. Except for a few European wines that are based on this action, carbon dioxide is not desirable in a table wine.

The timing of each of these operations, the temperatures, and the variations in procedures are all decided by the winemaker and his staff. These decisions are based upon tastings of each wine at every step in the process. Every wine is sampled every day by the laboratory and a full range of tests are made to determine the wine's condition. And during fermentation, a sample of every wine is taken every day — for tasting.

The results of the laboratory tests are entered into the computer and each morning's printout indicates the chemical condition and progress of each wine. Any unusual change is highlighted for quick observation by the enologists. But the chemical condition of wine says nothing about the taste of the wine. That requires a human palate. In addition to the daily computer printout specifying the physical and chemical condition of each wine the winemaker and enologists have a sample of each wine for appraising its color, aroma, and taste. These

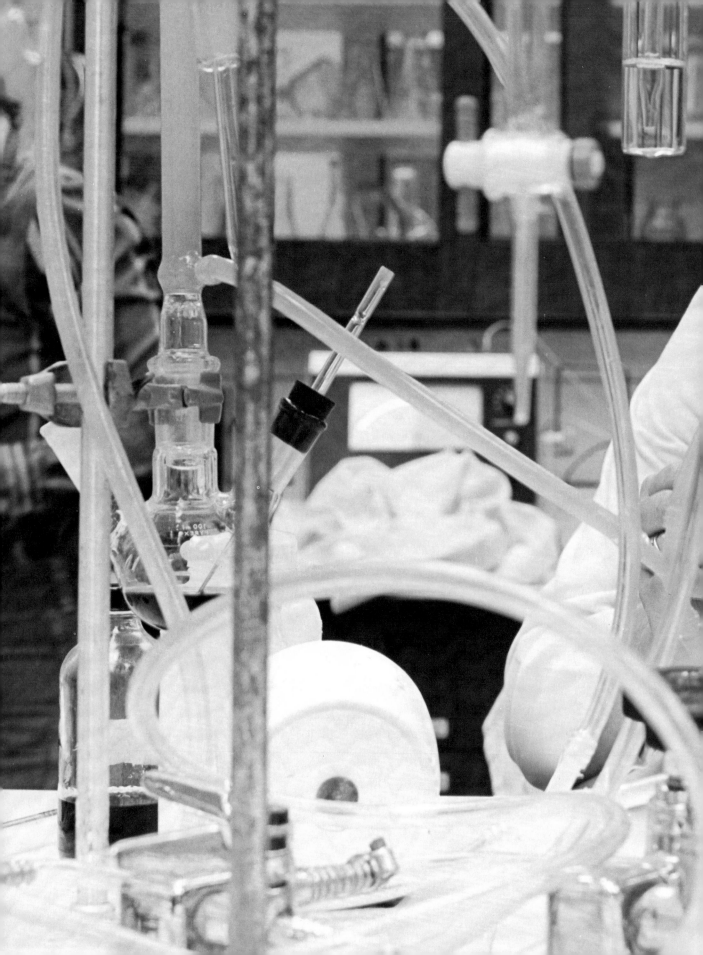

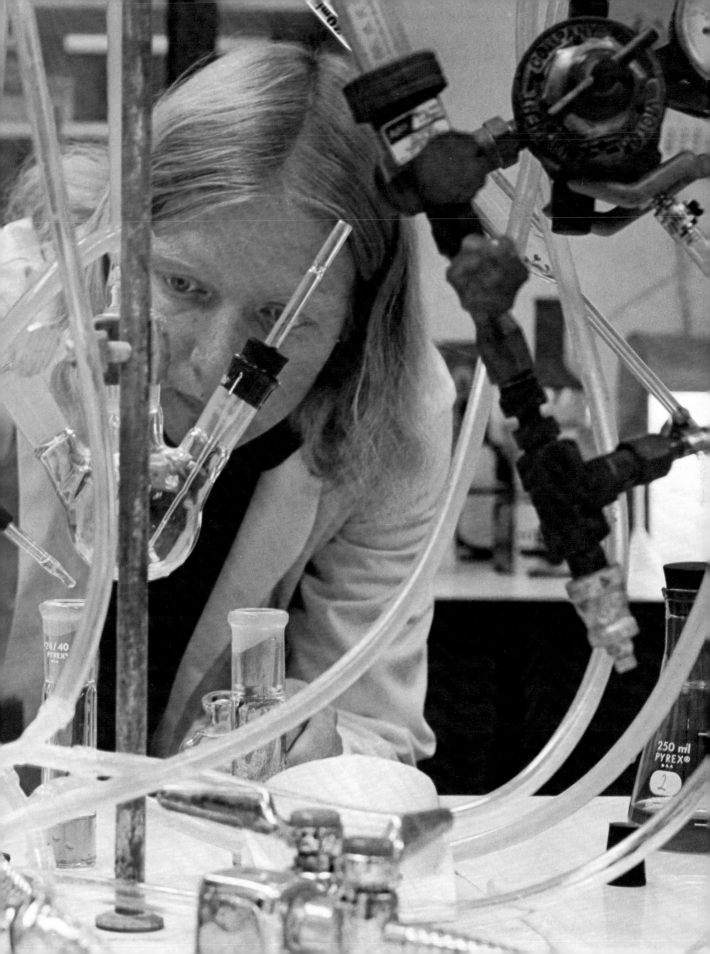

tastings determine when the wine is ready to move on to the next step and in many cases, what the next step will be.

After the fermentation and additional skin contact time is completed, the red wines are pressed. The procedure is the same as for the white wines. The free run, light press and heavy press juices are separated and then the free run and light press are blended. At this point the wine is likely to need to be clarified to remove any remaining yeast cells or other materials. This can be done in the centrifuge or by letting the wine settle in a tank and then drawing it off the top above the matter that has settled to the bottom. This is called racking — drawing the wine off the settled matter, off the "lees".

At this point the wine moves into aging containers. These may be large oak or stainless steel tanks, oak casks or barrels. The red wines move directly into sixty gallon oak barrels and the white wines go into oak casks or barrels, depending upon the variety. Except for Gamay Rose, all of the Robert Mondavi varietal wines spend some time in small oak storage. Robert Mondavi has long believed that small oak storage is of vital importance in bringing out the character and complexity of each wine. More on this in the next chapter.

Some of the wines moving into barrels are designated reserve. These are the best selections of those varieties from that vintage year. A wine meriting the reserve classification contains a character and a complexity that will mature only with time. It has within it a complex of acids and sugars, minerals and pigments, esters and aldehydes, and tannins. Only time will resolve these components into a harmonious whole.

Cabernet Sauvignon, Pinot Noir, Chardonnay and Fumé Blanc are wines with this reserve potential. These grapes extract more from their soils and the extended skin contact during and after fermentation transfers many more compounds into the wine. Over time, these compounds interact and mature, generating a richness and complexity of flavors that continue to reward the palate with a range of experiences. Tannin is the component that makes this long aging period possible. It is an oxygen inhibitor; without tannin, the wine would oxidize and die.

Unwanted oxygen is the enemy of the winemaker. It must be controlled every step of the way. The pressed juices are pumped into fermenting tanks through hoses designed to minimize oxidation and there are almost five miles of stainless steel inplace piping for moving wine throughout the winery. The pumps impelling the juices through the pipes are designed to minimize oxidation as well as agitation.

During fermentation there is so much carbon dioxide generated and bubbling up that there is no space for oxygen at the top of the tank. As the fermentation slows in its later stages it is necessary to monitor the tanks. As shown a few pages earlier, one of the laboratory group takes regular readings to detect any oxygen in the tops of the tanks. This anti-oxidation program carries on through the aging and bottling procedures. It never ends.

The cellarmaster tastes the juices at the press. His palate tells him where the baffle between the light and heavy presses should be located. This is done with all of the wines as they are pressed. As noted previously, tasting is the key operation in the winemaking process.

Each fermentation bung bubbling as the Chardonnay flows into the oak barrels to finish fermenting

the pumpover sends the skins and seeds
swirling through the fermenting wine

Later that morning, the cellarmaster will join the winemaker and the enologists in the tasting room. There they will appraise 137 samples collected from all of the tanks by the laboratory.

Fifty-five white wines and eighty-two red wines to be tasted, evaluated, discussed and acted on. Computer printouts tell of the temperatures, sugars, acids, rates of change and other data. A mass of numbers to be scanned quickly, searching for the un-predicted, for the deviation requiring immediate attention. The data then gets confirmation through tasting. A look at the figures and then a taste confirms the data but it also goes much further. The taste also provides an appraisal of the quality of the particular batch — where it is now and where it may be in time.

These judgments are made, compared, discussed; decisions are made. The decisions are responsible for the movement, the intensity, and the personal involvement taking place down in the cellar. The urgency of the crush provides further emphasis. The crusher-stemmer sends new batches of juice, skins, pulp, and seeds surging into holding tanks. The white press is running continuously. Of the 137 batches already in various stages of the winemaking process, a majority will require some action. Some will need to be racked and the lees shoveled out. Other will need to be pumped over. Still others will be pumped into barrels to complete the fermentation. Many will need to move through the presses.

To be in the cellar at that time is to see a group of concerned workers, very much involved in what they are doing and taking pains with the way it is done. The wine must be protected. The tank must be clean, not somewhat clean but really clean. The movement of the wine must be done efficiently with a minimum of delay. The operations are done by in-dividuals or teams of two workers and the visitor is struck by the amount of personal respon-sibility evident among the workers. It is obviously a responsibility to the job but it also is quite clear that there is a responsibility to the wine. And each wine is different.

Each wine has an identity and it soon acquires a history as it progresses through the winemaking process. It is known to the cellar workers. Part of the job of being a cellar worker is knowing the differences between wines, between Cabernet Sauvignon and Pinot Noir and all others, and what must be done to each wine. But a batch of wine is not merely Pinot Noir, it is a particular vintage Pinor Noir and it has its own particular character. The men and women working in the cellar and the barrel rooms know each of their wines and it shows in their work.

This involvement with each of the wines is given further encouragement through the weekly wine tastings. The winery's executives meet weekly for formal blind tastings, comparing their Robert Mondavi wines with competing wines both domestic and foreign. These tastings are then duplicated and opened to all employees. They provide a very direct measure of the value in treating each wine as a distinct entity with its own taste, its own character, its own reward to the palate.

The wine has been racked. The solids are gone. The sugars are gone. Now there are acids, flavors, alcohols, tannin and hundreds of other compounds, known and unknown. All will work with others in generating new compounds and new flavors as the wine is both protected by and interacting with oak — month after month after month.

Diener & Roth
Stuttgart

NO. 239
CAP. 338

OAK
CASK
STORAGE

R+SO₂ 35½
7-16 To

OAK PROVIDES AN IDEAL environment for nature to work its wonders in aging fine wines. Oak adds flavor to the wine while allowing oxygen to seep through its staves to play an active role in the aging process in softening the more astringent components. And its effects can be controlled through the size of the container.

The large oak tanks range in size from 1500 to 8000 gallons. Made of Yugoslavian oak, they are used primarily for fermentation and storage but they do provide an ideal place for the short aging period of Chenin Blanc. Two months in a large tank provides just the right touch of oak for this moderately sweet and fruity wine.

The same is true for German style wine. Johannisberg Riesling is aged for five months in the time-tested 300 and 600 gallon German white oak casks. Larger tanks would not have enough oak effect on the short aging of this light wine with its fragrant softness and the smaller barrels would overpower the fine flowery bouquet.

The character of the more complex wines is brought out by aging them in the small oak cooperage — the 60 gallon barrels. The small oak containers give the wine a character that can't be achieved by aging in the large tanks or casks. Because of this special character, the winery's barrel population is above 19,000 and growing by 2000 or so annually.

The choice of oak is another variable in the winemaking process. Different oak will produce different wines. The oak from the Nevers Forest near Bordeaux will have a different effect on the wine than the oak from the Limousin Forest which has a higher porosity and lower tannin. Both are French oaks but they have differing effects and both of these French oaks are different than the oak of Yugoslavia or Wisconsin or Illinois. Even the method for cutting the barrel staves plays a part. The taste will vary if the oak staves are split instead of quartersawn.

American oak has been used for a few vintages but most of the Mondavi barrels are made of the Nevers oak. The American barrel builders have been occupied making barrels for aging whiskies and they have developed their designs and techniques for that market. The growth of the wine industry in the past decade has required the winemakers to go to the wine barrel makers in France to fill their needs.

New barrels are needed every year for aging Chardonnay. The fullness, roundness and distinctive aroma of the Chardonnay grape are brought along by nine to twelve months in virgin oak barrels. Additional complexity is added by keeping the wine in contact with the yeast during the barrel aging.

With a barrel population above 19,000 and growing, the cooper's skills are in great demand. Trained in Bordeaux, he is kept occupied plying his ancient craft much as it has been done for centuries.

The light, golden-hued Fumé Blanc also benefits greatly from the small oak barrels. Early in the fermentation, five percent of the wine is transferred to French oak barrels. Another 25 to 30 percent of the wine goes directly to Nevers barrels after fermentation for aging in contact with the yeast. The balance is clarified and then put in the oak barrels for the eight to ten months aging. A roundness and richness develops in this wine that has great appeal when young and fruity and also has the ability to develop further for several years in the bottle.

hand turned for slow, even drying
two years in the open air —
French oak ready to do its work.

The small oak barrels perform their most masterly work in providing an aging environment for the complex red wines with their many additional extractions from the skins and seeds. Two years and more are required for the various compounds to do their work in softening the wine and bringing out its full complexity. Oxygen is also needed but at a very slow rate. The tannins in the aging wine inhibit enough of the oxygen coming through the oak to prevent the wine from becoming oxidized and spoiled. A balance is achieved. The wine has the time it needs in the oak for the various compounds to interact without any surplus of oxygen. Then when the wine is bottled, the oxygen supply is halted and the compounds continue their interactions for several years of bottle aging, increasing the softness, the fullness and the complexity. In the process, the tannins precipitate and become the sediment in the bottom of the bottle of an aged, fine wine.

The barrels have been washed and inspected; they are ready for the wine. The high speed pump pours 60 gallons into the barrel in a little more than two minutes. As the nozzle is moved to the next barrel, the space at the top is filled from the pitcher and wine splatters out as the bung is driven down. The entire space is filled with wine. The barrel is then rotated an eighth of a turn to keep the bung moist.

Just as the oak allows a very slow diffusion of oxygen through the barrel into the wine, it also allows a slow diffusion of water and alcohol outward. Space begins to form inside the barrel. This is called ullage. Air enters the barrel to fill the space. The ullage can have harmful effects on the wine if allowed to remain and expand. To avoid unwanted oxidation and possible bacterial activity, the barrel is "topped" with more of the same wine. This topping takes place regularly throughout the entire barrel aging period. It must be done more frequently, every other week or so, early in the aging period as the young wine cools in the cellar and then, as the aging process settles in, every few months is sufficient to keep the wine in healthy condition.

The forklift rises upward high above the truck to the top row of barrels and the prongs move inward and then up, lifting and then lowering the two barrels down to the aging room floor. The barrels are regularly brought down from their resting places and inspected before they are topped. Every barrel undergoes the critical eye and nose of the barrel enologist. A deep whiff at the bung hole, a flashlight on the wine — if all looks and smells well, the barrel is approved for topping. If the aroma of any barrel is different from the others, the wine is tasted by the enologist to determine its condition.

A wine can go either way as it ages. It can change from a reserve wine to a regular classification or it can develop beyond all expectations. Six months to a year can and often does make a large difference. Sometimes the difference is so great the enologist needs reinforcement to confirm his appraisal. He literally can't believe his own senses. Every wine travels its own path in the barrel and it needs to be monitored regularly. Its development will not be finished when it is bottled. The wine will develop as much in the bottle as it did in the barrel but by the time it is ready for bottling the final point is more predictable.

The continuing tastings determine the classification and the handling of the wine. The reserve wines will usually get additional aging in oak and special treatment prior to

bottling. In most cases, the reserve wines will not be fined nor will they be filtered.

Fining and filtering are two methods at the winemaker's disposal for removing unwanted substances in wines. Fining clarifies wine by the addition of an agent which produces a precipitate removing the unwanted substances which would not settle without the fining agent. Fining agents can be proteins such as egg whites, gelatin, casein or isinglas or they can be adsorbents such as the clayish mineral bentonite which will remove proteins in wine. There are other agents for special uses and winemakers and enologists are constantly testing different materials in the search for agents that will work selectively, removing particular substances while leaving those that give the wine its special character.

Filtering is done by passing the wine through membranes of varying porosity composed of inert cellulose stems. Filtering will remove particles such as yeast cells, other microbial cells or crystal-like precipitates. Filtering is especially important for the light wines with residual sugar — Johannisberg Riesling, Chenin Blanc, Gamay Rose — to avoid the possibility of fermentation of the residual sugar by yeast cells remaining in the wine after it has been bottled. The winemaker is able to control the degree of filtration to avoid removing the elements which give the wine its particular character.

Between the wide range of fining agents and the variety of filtration methods the winemaker has a wide range of options available for clarifying a wine. The condition of the particular wine determines which option will be used and when there are questions about which option will do a particular job, the answer can be found by carefully measured tests on small samples.

The bottling continues the struggle against unwanted oxidation and contamination. The wine travels under pressure from the bottling tank to the filler and into the bottles. If the wine is to age for any length of time in the bottle without becoming oxidized, the seal must be airtight and remain so. That is why wines are sealed with one and a half to two inch corks and why the bottles are laid on their sides keeping the corks moist. Even a two inch cork cannot keep the air out of the wine bottle if it is allowed to dry and shrink. The cork needs to be kept moist if it is to continue to press tightly against the inside of the neck of the bottle.

Bottling disturbs the wine and several weeks of settling are usually required for the wine to regain its delicate equilibrium. This is called "bottle shock" and it is further testimony to wine being alive. The recovery from bottle shock, however, is not the most important effect of bottle aging. The development of the wine's bouquet occurs then.

Underlying the winemaking procedures is an extensive experimental program. During the harvest, small batches of many grape varieties are crushed and kept in separate containers for fermentation and aging. Each batch tests the effect of some variable in methods of crushing, fermentation, cooperage, aging — every step in the winemaking process. Additional time on the skins, higher or lower fermentation temperatures, a different strain of yeast, another method of crushing, of pressing, of clarification; the variables are almost endless. Each particular experiment is intended to answer a question raised by one of the winemaking group, a question that emerged during the regular cellar and aging operations. The wines produced by these tests are blind tasted by the winemaking group and these tastings, sometimes covering a span of several years, determine whether that experimental procedure improved the wine and whether it should be incorporated into the full-scale operations. The research program and the tasting provide a considerable amount of direct experience with the consequences of altering many of the variables involved in winemaking.

The tastings lead to that final decision; release the wine. As discussed in the next chapter, some of the wines will be ready to be uncorked and enjoyed to the fullest. Others will be drinkable at release date but they will also improve in the bottle, some for as many as five years before they reach their peak. Once the wines are released, their nurture depends upon the interest and care of the consumer. Some ideas and information on gaining the fullest enjoyment from fine wines are presented in the next chapter.

The glass is filled with aroma and bouquet. The color pleases the eye, the fragrances excite the nose. Soon, the silky touch on the tongue and the fruity flavors on the palate. The senses experience another wine — the climax of the collaboration between the winemaker and the wine drinker.

THE DELICATE FLAVOR and velvety softness of Pinot Noir enhances the subtle aromas and flavors of chicken prepared in a pastry shell for Robert Mondavi and his luncheon guests in the winery's Vineyard Room.

A fine wine, like fine cuisine, music, and art, is both a sensuous and an intellectual experience. The senses are exercised and rewarded with fine stimulations; colors, aromas, flavors with subtle differences and similarities between this wine experience and other wine experiences. The mind is also exercised, consciously comparing this wine now and this wine six months ago or this wine and another wine of the same variety.

In all cases, wine tasting and appreciation involves and depends upon the recall of earlier experiences and the expectations created by the earlier experiences. As the glass of wine is raised, the mind is preparing the senses for the experience just as the forkful of Thanksgiving turkey is met by the remembrances of past Thanksgiving turkeys. What one expects to taste plays the greatest part in what is actually tasted. The effect of prior knowledge and the expectations it raises is so great that professionals taste "blind" when they are working. The identity of the wine being tasted is not known. When there is no prior knowledge of what is being tasted, the senses must provide all of the information.

The finer discriminations in wine tasting and drinking are dependent upon the same conditions as finer discriminations in cuisine, music, art, everything — interest and prior experience. As experience with wines multiplies, each wine adds to the wine drinker's memory and this growing store of experience makes the palate ever more sensitive and each new wine is then experienced ever more fully.

Experience not only increases the sensitivity for making finer discriminations, it greatly increases the pleasures. The subtleties, the nuances, the many complexities in fine wines begin to be consciously experienced. It is like the music student beginning to hear melody and perceive structure and relationships from what was previously an undistinguished sound. Wine drinking experience equips the wine drinker to collaborate with the winemaker in experiencing all of the dimensions of the fine wine which the winemaker's art has produced.

Tasting, as a separate activity, involves a particular sequence of sensory experience of the wine. Beginning with information available to the eyes, the wine is evaluated visually. Its appearance can reveal several important bits of information. The wine should be clear; any cloudiness indicates that something is wrong. Color can reveal the age of the wine. Brown indicates that the wine is old, and in red wines, blackish or purple colors indicate young wines which will need much time to mature.

With experience, the wine taster acquires a range of reference and the many tints and shades of wine become meaningful. Each can be judged against the norm for that variety. The taster evaluates the appearance of a wine by tipping the glass away and looking through the shallow edge on the far side of the glass, preferably against a white background. Fluorescent lighting should be avoided when possible; it alters the color. To lift a glass of wine and hold it to the light and experience fine color and body greatly increases the pleasure of drinking wine whether the purpose is to rigorously evaluate that wine or merely to enjoy it.

The second step in the tasting sequence is the most important — the odor of the wine. Odor is more important than taste because of the great variety of subtle odors found in wines and the capability of the nose to discriminate among them. There are only four basic tastes — sweet, sour, bitter, salt — which the tongue recognizes, whereas the olfactory nerve discriminates between thousands of different odors. Also, most of what we think of as a taste is actually smell. When we taste food, we are getting more information from the aroma of the food than from the actual taste on our tongues.

To enable the olfactory nerve to get the wine's full story, the wine taster swirls the wine in the glass and fills the bowl with its vapors. Then sniffing deeply, the taster brings the vapors up into the recesses of the nasal cavity. The odor of wines is divided into two types — aroma and bouquet. Aroma is the smell of the grape from which the wine was made and bouquet is the complex smell resulting from the many interactions taking place during fermentation and aging.

Describing the "nose" of a wine can be very trying. There is no precise vocabulary for denoting any of the more than 350 subtle odors of wines. We are required to use the names of other objects which emit the same odors. Thus, young wines which are redolent with the aroma of their grapes are usually described by such items as apples, grapes, peaches, spices and flowers whereas older wines with complex bouquets are likened to more earthy things such as mushrooms, nuts, coffee, heavier spices and even birds and animals. Briary, herbaceous, green-olive, weedy, minty, coffee-bean, earthy, grassy, peppery and prune-like are some of the terms that wine tasters have used to describe the bouquets of aged red wines. There seems to be no end to the associations made by sensitive wine tasters when consciously evaluating the aromas and bouquets of complex wines.

To get the most pleasure from the bouquet of a fine wine, the wine drinker will rotate the glass back and forth under the nose and inhale time and time again. The wine with a "long nose" will release its bouquet slowly and fully, flooding the nasal cavity with a host of delightful sensations.

The final step in tasting is a good mouthful of the wine, moved through every part of the mouth to get full contact. Then air is drawn in between the lips and through the wine, causing vapors to rise to the back of the mouth and to the nasal cavity. The tip of the tongue reveals whether the wine is sweet and the sides of the tongue up at the front pick up any saltiness. Further back, the sides of the tongue sense any sourness. Here is where the wine's acids are tasted. At the back of the tongue are the sensors for the bitter, which in wine indicates tannin. With the mouthful of wine, the body and the balance are experienced and terms like acid, flat, balanced, smooth, soft, rough, and elegant come into play. The elegant wine is everything a wine should be and the rough wine is just the opposite; a poor, badly made wine. The wine can be vigorous or flat, depending upon the amount of fruit acids present. The flat wine has little or no acid. The wine can be hard with much tannin, which is normal in a fine young red which needs aging, or it can be supple with a nice balance of alcohol and acidity and no excess tannin. The wine can have a lingering aftertaste, also called a long finish.

The Elements of Wine Appreciation

Wine engages the senses with color, scent, flavor, and texture.
The eyes, nose, palate, and touch are busy with:

a broad palette of brilliant hues and tints;

scents of spring flowers and the wood of the forests; and

tastes of the fruit and of the vine.

A host of pleasurable sensations.

At right, Michael Mondavi "noses" a Fumé Blanc, the golden-hued dry white wine with its distinctive varietal aroma and its full-bodied roundness. The happy marriage of fruit and oak enables Fumé Blanc to continue to grow in complexity for as many as six to eight years after bottling.

The mouthful of wine engages yet another of the five main senses — the sense of touch. The wine provides tactile sensations on the tongue and lining of the mouth; sensations which can vary greatly from wine to wine. These sensations can best be likened to those provided by fabrics or other materials whose surface qualities provide distinctive impressions to our sense of touch. It is not uncommon among tasters to describe a wine as being silky or coarse or woody or by some other textural quality which describes the sensation of the wine upon the surface of the mouth.

The only sense not directly stimulated by fine wine is the ear. Some wine drinkers will argue that wine does indeed stimulate the ear, that the sounds of a cork popping and of a fine wine flowing into the glass are important elements in the wine experience. They are akin to fine dinner music, setting up the anticipations and preparing the other senses for full experiences. For most wine drinkers, however, there is no question that fine wine does provide a wide range of sensations for four of the five main senses. Wine tasting engages sight, smell, taste, and touch to a greater degree than most things in life.

The ultimate goal of the wine tasting experience is the partnership of wine with food. Every fine food can find a suitable counterpart in wine. The flavors and substance of wine provide a balance to the flavors and substances of foods; a swallow of wine cleanses the palate, preparing it for another full experience of the particular food. The finely prepared fish in the butter sauce will be tasted fully again after a swallow of a light wine with its balance of fruit and acid. The aged cheese is perfectly balanced by the aged red wine while a light and young red wine enhances the flavors of roast turkey.

Which wine with which food? Just as the wine drinker learns which wines are most appreciated and best suit the drinker's palate only by tasting many wines, the questions of wine and food are best answered through experience. The age-old axioms of red wine with red meat and white wine with fish and poultry or sweet wines with dessert evolved in an earlier time when foods were prepared differently and wines were not made as well as today. These axioms can still be followed with many, many pleasing results but they can also be ignored just as many times with equally pleasing results.

Today's wines and today's methods for preparing foods provide an unlimited array of wine and food combinations. Light red wines are excellent with many kinds of fish and fruity red wines are a delight with many chicken recipes. Most wines will taste well with most foods, but for each palate, some wine and food combinations are special delights.

The ideal, as in all things, is to achieve a balance. Light and delicate foods are overpowered by intense wines. Fruity and fresh light wines would provide a better balance. Likewise, hearty foods can't be balanced by light wines; they call for the assertiveness of the fuller-bodied, aged wines — red or white. Experimentation is the way to knowledge

and then a few notations will avoid repeats of the less satisfying combinations and assure repeats of the special delights.

At left, Marcia Mondavi pours Napa Gamay to accompany a luncheon of cheeses and fruit. Smooth and medium-bodied with an outstanding aroma and flavor, the Napa Gamay complements the Brie, Fontina and Blue cheeses.

The serving of wine need not follow any rigid procedure. Wine has been served and consumed in every conceivable manner and with good results. There are no rules that need to be followed but there are a few common sense practices that will increase the enjoyment of wine.

Wine has been drunk out of every kind of vessel. Wood, metal, pottery, even animal skins are used to hold and serve wine but nothing works as well as a plain, stemmed glass with a rounded bowl. The clear, undecorated glass increases appreciation of the wine's color and brilliance and the rounded eight to ten ounce bowl handles a serving of wine with plenty of space above for the bouquet which is held in the glass by the slightly curved rim. This is the ideal all-purpose glass, working well for both red and white tables wines. The thinner the glass, the better the taste but it isn't necessary to spend a large amount of money for excellent glassware. As the appreciation of wine develops and expands into other types of wines, other sizes and styles of wine glasses can add to the wine drinker's enjoyment but there is no need to ever put the demand for the "proper" glass ahead of drinking and enjoying a good wine.

Since scent and flavor are most important in wine appreciation, it is critical that the glasses be free of any odor. They need to be rinsed carefully to remove all traces of detergent and they should be stored upright to avoid capturing and retaining any odor in the bowls.

The temperature of wine affects its taste and therefore is a factor in its appreciation. Aged red wines are at their best between 60 and 65 degrees Fahrenheit. Apparently this was room temperature in Europe during earlier times. In our heated homes, room temperatures of 68 to 75 degrees require red wines to be cooled slightly. Fifteen minutes in the door of the refrigerator should do the job nicely.

The complex dry white wines, such as Chardonnay and Fumé Blanc, are also at their best between 60 and 65 degrees instead of the 50 degrees traditionally recommended for white wines. The fruitier and lighter white wines, such as Johannisberg Riesling and Chenin Blanc, and rosé wines are better at the lower temperature of 50 degrees. Forty-five minutes to an hour in the refrigerator or fifteen minutes in an ice bucket will bring the white and rosé wines to temperature. Colder is not better. Ice cold wine loses its bouquet and, since most of the taste of wine derives from its fragrances, there will be little flavor to experience. Also, wine should never be heated to bring it up to temperature; that will destroy the wine. It is best for the wine to come up to temperature naturally by standing in the room.

As with all matters in appreciating wine, the wine drinker's palate is the only criterion. A little experimentation here also will be helpful. Drinking wines a little cooler or a little warmer than generally recommended may increase one's pleasure greatly. Many wine drinkers have found that they enjoy white wines when they are not as cold as the suggested 50 degrees and some of the lighter red wines when they are cooler than the usual 60 degrees.

Fine, aged red wines will most likely have a little sediment in them. Even after the wine is bottled, intricate chemical processes are going on very slowly. Some of the organic materials involved gradually combine into solids and they precipitate. The sediment doesn't affect the wine or its taste unless it is stirred back into the wine and drunk. Then the wine tastes unpleasant. To avoid that, let the wine stand for a couple of days or, if it is lying on its side, leave it in that position and, when the sediment is settled, pour the wine very slowly into a carafe or pitcher or another bottle, holding the neck of the bottle in front of a candle or light. When the first bit of sediment appears in the neck, stop pouring. That last swallow belongs in the sink.

At right, Tim Mondavi selects Fumé Blanc and Cabernet Sauvignon Reserve for a dinner party that evening. The Cabernet Sauvignon will be decanted into a carafe, leaving the sediment in the bottom of the bottle, and both wines will be chilled slightly.

There are a seemingly infinite number of instruments for uncorking a bottle of wine. The goal is to be able to uncork the wine slowly and carefully. The wing-type corkscrew works well because the cork moves upward while the pressure is being exerted downward. More and more widely used today is the double prong cork puller. Each prong is inserted between the cork and the bottle and then the two prongs are pushed down along the cork with an easy rocking motion. Then a twist with an upward pull slides the cork out of the bottle. The cork can also be replaced by reversing the process.

In pouring wine, it is best to hold the bottle close to the glass and pour it easily into the bowl. It is better to let the wine flow into the glass than to splash it down. The pouring of wine is a continuation of the care in handling wine generally. Wine does not respond well to harsh treatment and the better the wine, the more sensitive it is to abuse. No special techniques are required; wine doesn't have to be babied, only handled with some care.

If space is available, there are many advantages in storing wine instead of buying it only as needed. Your own wine cellar will provide an assurance of quality because of proper handling, the convenience of having the right wine when you want it and, finally, a considerable savings in cost.

In storing wine, you can be assured that the wine has received proper handling. Once the case is opened and the upside-down bottles taken out, the wine should be lying down. The corks will be moist and tight and no air will enter the bottles. Secondly, you are assured that there haven't been any large temperature variations. A cool temperature is preferable, 55 to 60 degrees, but more important than the exact temperature is that it is constant. If the storage place can be kept dark and free of strong odors, as from naptha, turpentine, heating oil, etc, so much the better. Finally, vibrations need to be avoided; the farther away from the refrigerator, furnace, and air conditioner motors, the better.

Given these few requirements — cool, dark, average humidity, no strong odors, lack of vibrations — it becomes evident that a wine cellar can be fit into a variety of loca-

102

tions in apartments as well as in houses. Depending upon the amount of wine to be cellared, suitable locations can be found in cabinets, pantries, closets, spaces under stairs and, in houses with basements, all kinds of places away from the furnace.

A simple home wine cellar is also a great convenience. It functions in the same manner as a well-stocked pantry, allowing a greater flexibility in menus and in impromptu entertaining. It provides assurance that the wine you want is there when you want it. It is another step in achieving the full pleasure of drinking fine wine.

Finally, when space is available, the home wine cellar can eventually provide the greatest of all wine experiences — fine red wines of full maturity — at a considerable savings in cost. The cellar can contain wines that need years of aging; years that can't be provided by the winery or the wine merchant without adding the storage costs to the price of the wine. To store a case of a full-bodied Cabernet Sauvignon or Pinot Noir for five years or more and then drink a bottle every six months and experience the wine and changes still taking place is to have what many wine lovers believe is the ultimate wine experience. It is experiencing everything the winemaker envisioned a decade or more earlier.

In an active collaboration with the winemaker by careful handling of the wines in storing and serving, the wine drinker is assured the full appreciation of all of the character and elegance developed in the wine by the winemaker's art.

The products of the winemaker's art at the Robert Mondavi Winery have been steadily approaching and reaching Robert's goal. Year by year, the wines are showing the results of the research, of the quality control in the vineyards and in the winery, and of the enthusiasm and energies at play guiding the wines from the crusher to the bottling room. Cabernet Sauvignon, Chardonnay, Fumé Blanc, Johannisberg Riesling, the list goes on and on; all winning gold medals in national and international blind tastings by world-renowned wine professionals. The list of awards is most impressive, not only for its length but for its breadth. Each of the Robert Mondavi varietal wines has been acknowledged to be among the leaders in its category and an amazing number of them, one year or another, have been judged to be among the top two or three in the world. Robert's wines are indeed competing favorably with the best wines the world can produce.

THIS BLESSED LAND

The cycle continues. The season is ended. The vines are pruned and they rest; conserving energy for the work to come. Another season; a cycle repeated thirty, forty, even fifty times before the vines are spent. Old vines are

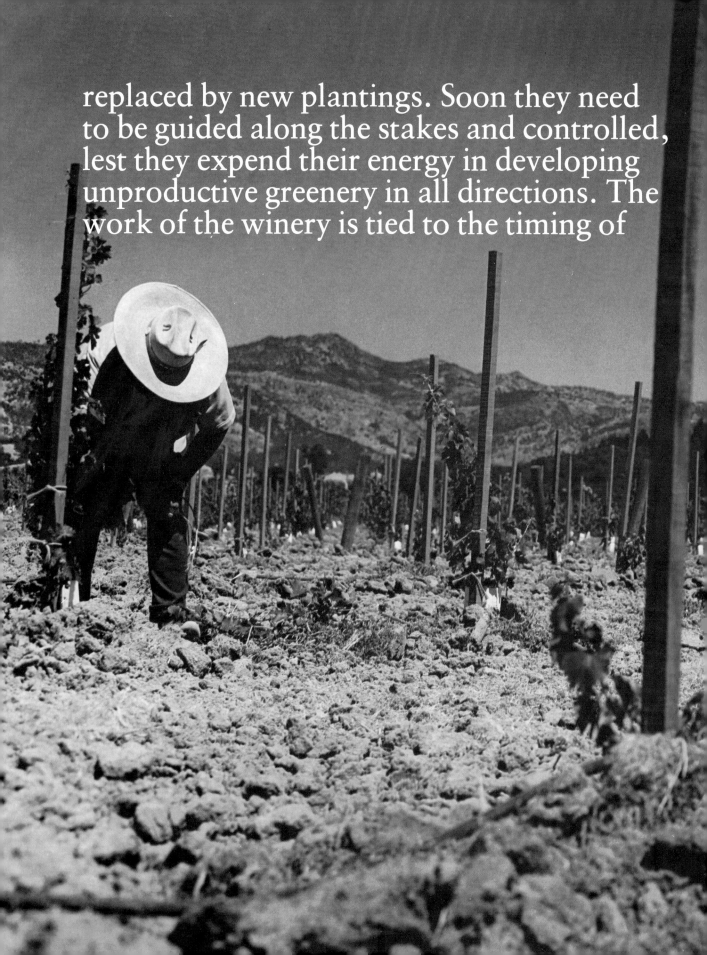

replaced by new plantings. Soon they need to be guided along the stakes and controlled, lest they expend their energy in developing unproductive greenery in all directions. The work of the winery is tied to the timing of

nature. Nature has its seasons in the vineyards where man waits upon the grapes and
nature has its time in the fermentation tanks
and in the aging cellars where man waits
upon the compounds to interact in a

continuing evolution of scents and flavors.
The winery tastes and waits, tastes and waits.
The wines are evolving—in their own time.
Some need to be moved, to be bottled; some
need more time in the wood. Only the palate

can determine which. The barrels multiply.
Month by month, year by year, they provide
the optimum environment for aging table
wines, for achieving the full development of
the character and the complexity of each wine.

To make the finest wines in the world is to enable nature to do its best work. It is a continuing challenge. One end is another beginning. The work goes on.